Teens' Basic Guide To Starting A Business

Teens' Basic Guide To Starting A Business

By Tocarra Eldridge-Robinson

Robinson Publishing, LLC
Contact: (312) 715-7884

Robinson Publishing, LLC
Published by Robinson Publishing, LLC

Copyright © 2023 by Robinson Publishing, LLC

Cover Design by Robinson Publishing, LLC
Art Direction by Aaron Robinson
Edited by Robinson Publishing, LLC

ISBN: 9798850758899

I would like to thank my loving and supportive husband, Aaron Robinson, whose love and guidance is with me in whatever I pursue. I would also like to thank my caring and compassionate mother, Lavern Eldridge, who has been a positive role model in my life. I am forever grateful for their unending inspiration.

TABLE OF CONTENTS

INTRODUCTION

Hey there! Are you tired of the same old routine? Do you dream of doing something different, something that really matters? Well, you're in luck, because this book is all about helping you start your own business and make your mark on the world.

Now, I know what you're thinking. "Starting a business? That sounds like something only adults do." But let me tell you, entrepreneurship is for everyone, including teenagers like you. In fact, some of the most successful businesses out there were started by people just like you - young, passionate, and full of ideas.

So, what exactly is entrepreneurship? Simply put, it's the act of creating something new and valuable that other people have interest in. It could be a product, a service, an app, or even a social cause. The point is, entrepreneurship is all about solving problems, making a difference, and creating a better future for yourself and others.

But let's not get ahead of ourselves. Starting a business can be a challenging and rewarding journey, and it all starts with a single step. In this book, we'll take that step together, exploring everything you need to know to get your business off the ground.

If you're ready to embark on a journey of creativity, innovation, and entrepreneurship, this book is for you. Let's get started, shall we?

The Author - T. Robinson

CHAPTER 1

Purpose of Starting a Business

Why do people decide to go into business?

Have you ever wondered why some people decide to start their own business? Well, there are many reasons why someone might take the leap into entrepreneurship.

For starters, **some people simply want to be their own boss**. They want to have more control over their work and their schedule, and they want to be able to make decisions that align with their values and goals. Others are **motivated by financial freedom**. Starting a successful business can be a way to build wealth and create opportunities for yourself and your family.

But, there's more to it than just independence and money. *Many entrepreneurs are driven by a desire to solve problems, create something new, or make a positive impact on the world.* They see a need or an opportunity that isn't being met, and they want to be the ones to fill that gap. For example, maybe you've noticed that there aren't many healthy food options in your school cafeteria, and you want to start a business that provides nutritious meals and snacks to students. Or maybe you're passionate about protecting the environment, and you want to create a company that develops sustainable products or services.

Whatever your motivation may be, starting a business can be a rewarding and challenging journey. It requires creativity, hard work, and a willingness to take risks and learn from failures. But if you're up for the challenge, entrepreneurship can be a way to turn your dreams into reality and make a difference in the world. So, if you have an idea or a passion that you want to pursue, don't be afraid to give it a shot!

What is the purpose of starting a business

Starting a business can have many different purposes, depending on the individual entrepreneur and the nature of the business. However, some common purposes that teenagers might have for starting a business include:

1. *To solve a problem:*

Many successful businesses start by identifying a need or a problem in the market that isn't being adequately addressed. The entrepreneur sees an opportunity to create a product or service that will meet that need, and decides to start a business to fill the gap.

2. *To pursue a passion:*

Sometimes, teenagers start businesses simply because they're passionate about a particular product or industry. They want to create something that they believe in and that reflects their values and interests.

3. *To make a difference:*

For some entrepreneurs, starting a business is a way to have a positive impact on the world. They want to create a company that does good, whether that's by creating sustainable products, supporting local communities, or promoting social justice.

4. *To achieve financial freedom:*

Starting a successful business can be a way to build wealth and create financial security for yourself and your family.

Whatever your purpose for starting a business may be, it's important to remember that entrepreneurship is a journey that requires hard work, persistence, and a willingness to learn and adapt. But if you're passionate about your idea and committed to making it succeed, starting a business can be a fulfilling and rewarding experience that allows you to pursue your goals and make a difference in the world.

The kind of business you can go into

As a teenager who is interested in starting a business, you may be wondering what type of business you should pursue. The truth is, there are many different types of businesses that you can start, and the best option for you will depend on your interests, skills, and goals.

One popular option for teenage entrepreneurs is **selling products**. This can include anything from handmade crafts and jewelry to vintage clothing and electronics. If you're creative and enjoy making things, selling products can be a fun and rewarding way to start your own business.

Another option is to use your skills or trade to **offer a service**. For example, if you're good at fixing computers or smartphones, you could start a business offering tech support and repairs. Or if you're an excellent writer or graphic designer, you could offer your services to clients looking for content or branding help.

Starting an online business is also a popular option for teenage entrepreneurs. This could include anything from starting a blog or YouTube channel to selling products through an online store. With the rise of social media and e-commerce platforms, it's easier than ever to start an online business and reach a global audience.

Of course, there are many other types of businesses that you can start as a teenager. Some people start businesses based on a particular hobby or interest, such as baking, gardening, or photography. Others start businesses that address a particular need or gap in their community, such as a tutoring or pet-sitting service.

Ultimately, the key to choosing the right business for you is to think about your interests, skills, and goals. What are you passionate about? What are you good at? What do you want to achieve with your business? Once you've answered these questions, you can start to explore different business ideas and figure out which one is the best fit for you.

So, whether you're interested in selling products, using your skills to offer a service, starting an online business, or exploring other options, there are many possibilities for teenage entrepreneurs. The key is to stay curious, keep learning, and never be afraid to try something new. With the right mindset and a willingness to take action, you can start your own successful business and make a difference in the world.

CHAPTER 2

Seek Guidance and Counseling

Seek guidance from a mentor

One of the best things you can do is seek guidance from someone who has already gone through the process of starting a business. A mentor, someone who has started or is successful at a business like yours, can be an invaluable resource as you navigate the ups and downs of entrepreneurship. A mentor can provide you with insights and advice on everything from identifying your target market and setting prices to marketing your products and managing your finances. They can also offer encouragement and support when you hit roadblocks or face challenges along the way.

So, how do you find a mentor? *One way is to start by networking and reaching out to people in your community who have experience in the type of business you want to pursue.* This could include local business owners, entrepreneurs, or professionals who work in related industries. Another option is to *look for mentorship programs or organizations that connect young entrepreneurs with experienced business leaders.* For example, the Small Business Association (SBA) and SCORE both offer mentorship programs that can help you connect with experienced business owners and gain valuable guidance and support.

Once you've identified a potential mentor, it's important to approach them in a respectful and professional manner. Explain your goals and your interest in starting a business, and ask if they would be willing to provide you with guidance and support. Be prepared to listen and learn from their experiences, and be open to feedback and constructive criticism.

Of course, before you can seek out a mentor or start a business, it's important to know what type of business you want to pursue. This can involve researching different industries and business models, as well as identifying your own skills, interests, and passions.

One way to get started is to **visit a business center or small business association, such as the SBA or SCORE,** to learn more about the different types of businesses that are out there and what it takes to start and run a successful business. These organizations can provide you with resources, tools, and guidance to help you develop a business plan, secure funding, and navigate the legal and regulatory requirements of starting a business.

Another option is to talk to other entrepreneurs and business owners in your community and ask for their advice and insights. They may be able to provide you with valuable information about what it takes to succeed in their industry, as well as tips and strategies for starting and growing your own business.

Ultimately, the key to starting a successful business as a teenager is to stay curious, stay motivated, and stay focused on your goals. Seek out guidance and support from mentors and other resources, and be willing to put in the hard work and persistence needed to turn your dreams into a reality. With the right mindset and the right support, you can start your own successful business and make a difference in the global environment.

Knowing the operational cost to operate your business
To set effective goals, it's important to have a clear understanding of what it takes to start and run a

successful business. This involves not only understanding your target market and the needs and desires of your customers, but also having a grasp on the operational costs and requirements of your business. This includes everything from the cost of materials and labor to the cost of marketing and advertising, rent or lease expenses, insurance, taxes, and more. By having a thorough understanding of your operational costs, you can ensure that you set realistic goals that align with your financial resources and capabilities.

To learn more about what it takes to operate your business, it can be helpful to do research and seek guidance from resources like business centers, small business associations, and industry experts. These resources can provide you with valuable insights and advice on everything from financing and accounting to marketing and customer service.

It's important to stay up-to-date on industry trends and best practices, as well as to continually seek feedback and insights from your customers and other stakeholders. By staying informed and engaged, you can better position yourself to achieve your goals and build a successful, sustainable business.

Knowing your short-term and long-term goals
When it comes to starting a business, setting clear goals is crucial. This means identifying what you hope to achieve with your business, both in the short-term and in the long-term.

Short-term goals might include things like launching your product or service, building a customer base, and generating revenue. Long-term goals might involve expanding your business, building a brand, and achieving financial stability and success.

Long-term goals are the milestones you want your business to achieve in the future. It's important to have a clear understanding of what these goals are, as they will help you stay focused on your business's growth and development. How to create long-term goals:

1. Set realistic goals: Your goals should be challenging, but also achievable.
2. Be specific: Make sure your goals are clear and specific, so you can measure progress towards them.
3. Set a timeline: Determine when you want to achieve your goals, and create a plan to work towards them.
4. Consider your values: Your long-term goals should align with your business's values and mission.

For example, if you're starting a catering business, your long-term goals might include expanding your menu, opening a physical location, and hiring a team of employees.

CHAPTER 3

How to Decide on Services to Provide

Brainstorming different ideas and knowing your target market

Deciding on the service that you would like to provide is an important step when starting a business. Your service should be something that you are passionate about and that you have expertise in. This will make it easier for you to market your service and establish yourself as a leader in your industry.

To determine the type of service you would like to provide, **you can start by brainstorming different ideas and assessing your skills and interests**. You can also consider factors like market demand, competition, and profitability to narrow down your options and identify the most promising opportunities.

Once you have a clear idea of the service you would like to provide, the next step is to **define your target market**. Your target market is the group of customers that your service is specifically designed to serve. To define your target market, you should consider factors like demographics, geographic location, interests, and buying habits.

One effective way to define your target market is to create a customer persona. A customer persona is a detailed profile of your ideal customer, including their age, gender, income, interests, and more. By creating a customer persona, you can better understand the needs and preferences of your target market and tailor your service to meet their specific needs.

Another key factor to consider when defining your target market is your unique selling proposition (USP). Your USP is what sets you apart from your competitors and makes your service stand out in the marketplace. By identifying your USP and highlighting it in your marketing and advertising, you can attract customers who are specifically interested in the unique benefits that your service provides.

Deciding on the service you would like to provide and defining your target market are essential steps when starting a business. By carefully assessing your skills, interests, and market demand, and creating a detailed customer persona, you can position yourself for success and build a loyal customer base that will support your business endeavor.

What is your startup cost?
Starting a business requires resources, and one of the key resources you'll need to consider is your startup costs. These are the costs associated with getting your business up and running, and they can vary widely depending on the type of business you're starting and the resources you have at your disposal. You may also consider **borrowing money from a bank or other financial institution, or taking out a loan**. This can be a good option if you need a significant amount of capital upfront and are willing to take on some debt in order to achieve your business goals.

Regardless of which option you choose, it's important to have a clear understanding of your startup costs and to *create a detailed budget for your business*. This can help you to identify any potential funding gaps or areas where you may need to cut back on expenses in order to stay within your budget.

When it comes to funding your startup costs, there are several options to consider. One option is to **use your own savings or personal funds** to finance your business. This can be a good option if you have enough money saved up and feel comfortable investing your own resources into your business.

Another option is to **raise funds from friends and family members who believe in your business idea and are willing to invest in your success**. This can be a good way to get your business off the ground without taking on too much debt or risking your own financial stability.

Some common startup costs to consider include:
- **Business registration and legal fees:** This can include things like registering your business, obtaining licenses and permits, and paying for legal advice.
- **Equipment and supplies:** Depending on the type of business you're starting, you may need to purchase equipment, machinery, and supplies to get started.
- **Marketing and advertising:** This includes things like website development, social media advertising, and other promotional activities to help get the word out about your business.
- **Rent and utilities:** If you need a physical location for your business, you'll need to consider the costs of rent, utilities, and other expenses associated with operating a physical space.
- **Inventory and raw materials:** If you're selling a product, you'll need to purchase inventory and raw materials in order to produce your goods.

By taking the time to carefully consider your startup costs and identify potential funding sources, you can set yourself up for success as a young entrepreneur. With a clear understanding of your finances and a solid plan for achieving your business goals, you can build a successful, sustainable business that makes a real impact in society.

CHAPTER 4

Creating a Business Name

Brainstorming business name ideas

Brainstorming is a fun and creative process that can help you come up with a name that reflects your brand values and resonates with customers. The first step in brainstorming business name ideas is to gather a team of people who can offer different perspectives and ideas. This could include friends, family, or business partners who can offer valuable input. You may also want to consider hiring a branding or marketing expert who can help guide you through the process.

Once you have your team in place, it's time to start brainstorming. **One effective technique is to use a word association tool**. This involves writing down a list of words that relate to your business or brand, and then brainstorming related words or phrases. For example, if you're starting a fitness brand, you might start with words like "health," "wellness," and "exercise," and then brainstorm related words like "strength," "endurance," and "vitality."

Another technique is to use a name generator tool. These are online tools that can help you come up with unique and creative business names. Simply enter some information about your business, and the tool will generate a list of potential names. While these tools can be helpful, it's important to use them as a starting point and not rely on them too heavily.

When brainstorming business name ideas, it's important to keep your brand values in mind. **Think about what makes your business unique and what sets you apart from competitors**. This can include your mission, vision, and values, as well as your products or services. A good business name should reflect these values and communicate to customers what your business is all about.

It's also important to think about your target audience. Who are your ideal customers? What language and tone will resonate with them? Consider creating customer personas to help you better understand your audience and their needs.

When brainstorming business name ideas, **don't be afraid to think outside the box.** Consider using puns, alliteration, or other literary devices to make your name more memorable. You may also want to consider using a name that's inspired by your personal story or background. This can help create a deeper connection with customers and make your brand more authentic.

The importance of choosing the right business name
Choosing the right business name is crucial for the success of any business. Not only does a good name help you stand out from competitors, but it can also make a lasting impression on customers and convey your brand identity. In this section, we'll discuss the importance of choosing the right business name and offer some tips to help you come up with a name that will work for your brand.

First and foremost, **a good business name should be memorable**. It should be easy to remember and pronounce so that customers can easily recall it when they need your products or services. A memorable name can also help create brand recognition, which is essential for building a loyal customer base.

Your **business name should also reflect your brand values**. It should communicate to customers what your business is all about and what you stand for. This can include values such as quality, affordability, innovation, sustainability, or anything else that sets your business apart from competitors. A well-chosen name can help you create an emotional connection with your customers, which is essential for building brand loyalty.

Another important consideration when choosing a business name is to **make sure it's unique.** You don't want to choose a name that's already taken or is too similar to another business's name. This can lead to confusion among customers and legal issues down the road. Before settling on a name, make sure to conduct a thorough search to ensure it's available and not already trademarked.

When brainstorming business name ideas, it's important to think outside the box. Don't be afraid to get creative and come up with names that are catchy, memorable, and reflect your brand values. Brainstorming sessions can be a great way to generate a wide range of ideas. Encourage your team to think freely and come up with as many ideas as possible, without judging or dismissing any of them.

Once you've come up with a list of potential business names, it's important to evaluate each one carefully. *Consider factors such as how easy the name is to remember, how well it communicates your brand values, and how well it will work across different marketing channels.* You want a name that's versatile and can be used on your website, social media, business cards, and other marketing materials.

It's also important to test your chosen name in the real world. Share it with friends, family, or potential customers to get feedback. Does the name resonate with them? Does it accurately reflect your brand values? Is it easy to remember? Take their feedback into consideration and refine your name accordingly.

Finally, once you've settled on a name, *it's important to register it properly*. This can include filing for a DBA ("doing business as") if you're operating under a different name than your legal name, registering a trademark if you want to protect your brand name, and ensuring you've followed any legal requirements in your state or country.

Conducting a name availability search

Choosing a business name is an important step in starting a business, but it's not the end of the process. Once you've come up with a list of potential names, it's time to start evaluating them to determine which one is the best fit for your brand. In this section, we'll explore some key factors to consider when evaluating business name ideas.

The first factor to consider is brand uniqueness. You want your business name to stand out from competitors and be memorable to customers. To evaluate uniqueness, start by doing a Google search for each potential business name. Are there other businesses with the same or similar name? If so, it may be best to avoid that name to avoid confusion for customers.

The second factor to consider is domain name availability. Ideally, you want to choose a business name that has an available domain name so that customers can easily find your website online. Check domain name availability for each potential name using a domain registrar like GoDaddy or Namecheap.

The third factor to consider is the legal implications of your business name. Before finalizing a name, do a trademark search to ensure that it's not already trademarked by another business. This can help you avoid potential legal issues down the road. Ensure you think about how your business name will be perceived by customers. Does it accurately reflect your brand values and mission? Will it resonate with your target audience? Consider getting feedback from potential customers to help you evaluate the appeal of each potential business name.

After deciding on which name is best, be sure to ask yourself this question: Will your business name still be relevant and appropriate as your business evolves? Think about the long-term potential of each possible business name, look in different contexts; will it be easy to read and remember? Will it look good on a website or social media profile? Consider different visual presentations of your business name to ensure that it's visually appealing and recognizable.

CHAPTER 5

Legal Structure and Model

Choosing the right legal structure

Choosing the right legal structure for your business might sound like a fancy term, but it's really just a way of deciding how your business will be set up and run. Think of it like building a house - before you can start adding furniture and decorations, you need to decide what kind of foundation you want to build on.

There are a few different types of legal structures you can choose from, depending on what kind of business you're starting and how you want to run it. For example, if you're starting a lemonade stand with your friends, you might want to consider a partnership - this is where two or more people own the business together and share the profits and responsibilities. And if you're planning to start a larger business with employees and investors, you might want to consider incorporating your business as a corporation. This can provide more legal protections and allow you to raise money by selling shares of your company.

Each legal structure has its own pros and cons, so it's important to do your research and choose the one that best fits your needs. But don't worry - you don't have to figure it all out on your own! You can talk to a lawyer or seek legal counseling to help you make the right decision for your business.

Protecting Your Business

Protecting your business might not be the first thing on your mind when starting out, but it's important to think about if you want to make sure your hard work and ideas are safe. **There are a few different ways to protect your business legally, like patents, copyrights, and trademarks:**

PATENT
A patent is a legal protection for an invention or idea that you've come up with. This means that no one else can make, use, or sell your invention without your permission. If you've come up with a cool new gadget or technology, getting a patent might be a good idea to make sure no one else can copy your idea.

COPYRIGHT
A copyright is a legal protection for creative works like books, music, and art. This means that you have the exclusive right to make copies, distribute, or perform your work. If you're a musician or artist, getting a copyright can help make sure your work is protected and that you get credit for your creations.

TRADEMARK
A trademark is a legal protection for a brand name, logo, or slogan. This means that no one else can use your branding to sell their own products or services. If you've come up with a catchy name or logo for your business, getting a trademark can help make sure no one else can use it.

Each type of legal protection has its own rules and requirements, so it's important to do your research and make sure you qualify. But if you do, it can be a great way to protect your business and your ideas.

Compliance with Laws and Regulations
Complying with laws and regulations might not be the most exciting part of starting a business, but it's important to make sure you're following the rules. **There are a lot of laws and regulations that businesses have to comply**

with, like tax laws, labor laws, and environmental regulations:

Tax laws
Tax laws are probably the ones you're most familiar with - these are the rules about how much money you have to pay to the government from your business profits. Depending on where you live and what kind of business you have, there might be different taxes you have to pay or forms you have to fill out.

Labor laws
Labor laws are the rules about how you treat your employees. This includes things like minimum wage, overtime pay, and workplace safety. If you're planning on hiring employees for your business, you'll need to make sure you're following these laws to avoid getting in trouble.

Environmental regulations
Environmental regulations are the rules about how you impact the environment. Depending on what kind of business you have, you might need to make sure you're not polluting the air or water, or that you're disposing of waste properly.

There are a lot of different laws and regulations to keep track of, but don't worry - there are resources out there to help you. You can talk to a lawyer or accountant to make sure you're in compliance, or check out government websites for more information. By following the rules, you can make sure your business is successful and responsible at the same time.

CHAPTER 6

Writing and Developing a Business Plan

Starting a business can be a rewarding adventure, but it can also be overwhelming. One of the most important things you can do to set yourself up for success is to create a business plan. A business plan is like a roadmap for your business - it helps you figure out where you're going and how to get there. Here's a step-by-step guide to writing and developing a business plan:

1. **Start with an executive summary:** The first part of your business plan should be an executive summary. This is like an introduction to your business plan, and should be a brief summary of what your business is all about. It should include your mission statement, a brief description of your product or service, and your goals for the business.

2. **Describe your business next**: You should describe your business in more detail. This section should include information about what kind of business you're starting, what products or services you'll offer, and what sets your business apart from competitors.

3. **Conduct market research:** Before you can start selling your product or service, you need to make sure there's a market for it. Conducting market research can help you figure out who your customers are, what they need, and how you can best serve them. This section should include information about your target market, your competitors, and your marketing strategies.

4. **Outline your organizational structure**: In this section, you should outline how your business will be structured. This includes information about who will be in charge of what, what kind of employees

you'll need, and how you'll manage finances and other aspects of the business.

5. ***Develop a financial plan:*** One of the most important parts of your business plan is your financial plan. This section should include information about how much money you'll need to start the business, how you'll fund the business, and how you'll make money. It should also include financial projections for the first few years of the business, including sales and expenses.

6. ***Describe your products or services:*** This section should go into more detail about the products or services you'll be offering. It should include information about how you'll create or source your products, what makes them unique, and how you'll market and sell them.

7. ***Create a marketing plan:*** In this section, you should outline your marketing strategies for your business. This includes information about how you'll reach your target market, what kind of advertising and promotion you'll use, and how you'll measure the success of your marketing efforts.

8. ***Outline your operations plan:*** This section should include information about how you'll run the day-to-day operations of your business. It should include details about how you'll manage inventory, how you'll fulfill orders, and how you'll manage customer service.

9. ***Add supporting documentation:*** Finally, you should include any supporting documentation that will help back up your business plan. This might include financial statements, legal documents, or other important information.

Writing a business plan can be a lot of work, but it's an important step in starting a successful business. By following these steps and taking the time to think through each aspect of your business, you'll be setting yourself up for success. Remember, starting a business is a journey, and a solid business plan can be your roadmap to success.

When starting a business, it's important to have a clear idea of what your company stands for and who your target audience is. One way to do this is by creating a tagline, mission statement, and statement of purpose. Here's how to create these essential elements of your business, and how to identify your target audience.

How to create a tagline
A tagline is a short, catchy phrase that sums up what your business is all about. It should be memorable and communicate your brand's unique value proposition. Here are some tips for creating a tagline:
1. Keep it short and sweet: A tagline should be no more than a few words or a short phrase.
2. Make it memorable: Use creative language and humor to make your tagline memorable.
3. Communicate your brand's value proposition: Your tagline should sum up what makes your business unique.

For example, if you're starting a bakery that specializes in gluten-free treats, your tagline might be "Delicious treats, no gluten."

How to create a mission statement
A mission statement is a statement of your business's purpose and values. It should be concise, easy to

understand, and communicate what your business does and why it exists. Here are some tips for creating a mission statement:

1. Start with your "why": Begin your mission statement by explaining why your business exists.
2. Keep it concise: A mission statement should be no more than one or two sentences.
3. Use clear language: Your mission statement should be easy to understand and communicate what your business does.

For example, if you're starting a social media marketing agency, your mission statement might be "Our mission is to help businesses grow by creating engaging, effective social media strategies."

How to create a statement of purpose
Creating a statement of purpose: A statement of purpose is a more detailed explanation of what your business does and what you hope to achieve. It should be a longer document than your mission statement, and should include more detail about your business's goals and values. Here are some tips for creating a statement of purpose:

1. Start with your mission statement: Use your mission statement as a starting point for your statement of purpose.
2. Include details about your products or services: Explain what your business does and how you plan to do it.
3. Explain your values: Include information about your business's values and how they guide your decision-making.

For example, if you're starting a clothing brand that uses sustainable materials, your statement of purpose might include information about your commitment to reducing your environmental impact and how you plan to source materials ethically.

How to identify your target audience

Knowing your target audience is essential for creating effective marketing campaigns and building a loyal customer base. Here's how to identify your target audience:

1. Define your product or service: Start by defining what your business offers and what problems it solves.
2. Identify your ideal customer: Think about who your ideal customer is and what their needs and interests are.
3. Research your market: Conduct market research to identify trends and patterns in your industry.
4. Analyze your competitors: Look at your competitors and see who their target audience is.

For example, if you're starting a skincare brand that specializes in natural, organic products, your target audience might be environmentally conscious women between the ages of 25 and 40 who prioritize natural ingredients in their skincare routine. By understanding your target audience, you can create marketing campaigns that speak directly to their needs and interests.

CHAPTER 7

Marketing and Promotion

Marketing and promoting your business is essential for reaching your target audience and generating revenue. Follow these steps to effectively market and promote your goods and services:

1. Define your brand: Create a clear and consistent brand identity that communicates what your business is all about.
2. Use social media: Social media is a powerful tool for reaching your target audience and promoting your goods and services.
3. Partner with influencers: Consider partnering with influencers in your industry to promote your business to a wider audience.
4. Offer promotions and discounts: Offer promotions and discounts to incentivize customers to try your goods and services.

For example, if you're starting a fitness studio, you could define your brand as a welcoming and inclusive community that prioritizes holistic health. You could use social media platforms like Instagram and TikTok to showcase your studio's workouts and share tips for healthy living. You could also partner with local health and wellness influencers to promote your studio to their followers, and offer a discount on your first class to incentivize new customers to try your studio.

How to Create Stationary Material
When it comes to marketing and promoting your business, creating stationary material like letterheads, business cards, and emails can help establish your brand identity and make a lasting impression on potential customers. Here are some tips for creating effective stationary material:

1. *Design a logo:* Your logo is the visual representation of your brand, so it's important to create one that is memorable and reflective of your business. Consider working with a graphic designer or using online logo design tools to create a professional-looking logo.
2. *Choose a color scheme:* Select a color scheme that aligns with your brand's personality and values. This color scheme can be used consistently across all of your stationary material to create a cohesive and recognizable brand identity.
3. *Create a letterhead:* A letterhead is a sheet of paper with your business's name, logo, and contact information printed at the top. This stationary material can be used for formal communication like business letters, invoices, and contracts. Make sure your letterhead design is consistent with your brand identity and includes all necessary contact information.
4. *Design business cards:* Business cards are a great way to introduce yourself and your business to potential customers. Make sure your business card design is eye-catching and includes your logo, contact information, and a brief description of your goods or services.
5. *Create a professional email signature:* Your email signature should include your name, job title, and contact information. You can also include a link to your business's website or social media profiles to encourage customers to learn more about your business.

By creating professional-looking stationary material, you can establish your brand identity and make a positive impression on potential customers. Make sure to use consistent branding across all of your stationary material to create a cohesive and recognizable brand identity.

How to Advertise Your Business
Spread the Word on Various Platforms: As a teenager starting a business, it's important to get the word out about your goods or services. Advertising can help you reach potential customers and grow your business. Here are some tips on how to advertise your business:

1. **Spread the word:** The first step in advertising your business is to let people know about it. Share your business with your family, friends, and community members. Attend local events and networking opportunities to meet new people and spread the word about your business.

2. **Use social media:** Social media is a powerful tool for advertising your business. Create profiles on platforms like Instagram, Facebook, Twitter, and LinkedIn, and regularly share updates and promotions with your followers. Use hashtags to increase the reach of your posts and engage with your audience by responding to comments and messages.

3. **Advertise on radio:** Local radio stations often offer affordable advertising packages for small businesses. Create a catchy jingle or commercial that promotes your business and reaches your target audience. Make sure to include your contact information and a clear call-to-action in your ad.

4. **Utilize newspapers:** Consider placing an ad in your local newspaper to reach a wider audience. Make sure to create an eye-catching design and include all necessary contact information. You can also

consider offering a special promotion or discount for readers who mention the ad when they contact your business.

5. **Create community flyers:** Design and print flyers to distribute in your community. Include your business name, logo, and contact information, as well as a brief description of your goods or services. Distribute these flyers at local events, community centers, and public spaces.

By utilizing a variety of advertising platforms, you can reach a wider audience and grow your business. Make sure to track the success of your advertising efforts and adjust your strategy accordingly. With persistence and a solid advertising strategy, your business can thrive.

How to Build a Website and Purchase Paraphernalia for Your Business

As a teenager starting a business, having a website can help establish your brand and reach potential customers. In today's digital age, having a website is essential for any business. A website serves as an online storefront and can help you reach a wider audience. Here are some tips on how to build a website for your business:

1. Choose a domain name: Choose a domain name that represents your business and is easy to remember. Make sure to check if it's available and purchase it from a domain registrar like GoDaddy or Namecheap.
2. Use a website builder: There are many website builders available online, such as website builders like Wix, Squarespace, or WordPress to create your website. These platforms offer user-friendly templates and drag-and-drop interfaces that make

it easy to design and customize your site. Choose a website builder that is easy to use and fits your budget.

3. <u>Add content:</u> Add content to your website, including information about your business, products or services, contact information, and testimonials from satisfied customers. Your website should include a homepage, an about page, a services or products page, and a contact page. Create high-quality content that accurately reflects your business and services.

Purchase paraphernalia: Purchase paraphernalia for your business, such as business cards, banners, flyers, and other promotional materials. Make sure to use your business name and logo on all of these materials to establish your brand. Paraphernalia such as t-shirts, mugs, and tote bags can also help promote your business. Purchase items with your business logo and website address and give them out to customers as a promotional item.

Tips to Giving out Discounts
Giving out discounts can be a great way to attract new customers and retain existing ones. Here are some tips on how to give out discounts:

1. *Set clear terms:* Set clear terms for your discounts, including the amount, duration, and any restrictions or limitations.

2. *Use social media:* Use social media to promote your discounts and encourage followers to share with their networks.

3. *Reward loyal customers:* Offer special discounts or promotions to loyal customers to show your appreciation.

4. *Offer seasonal discounts:* Offer discounts during holidays or special events to attract customers who are looking for deals.

5. *Offer referral discounts:* Encourage customers to refer their friends and family to your business by offering them a discount on their next purchase.

How to Join Business Clubs and Associations

Joining business clubs and associations can help you connect with other entrepreneurs and gain valuable insights and resources. Here's how to join:

1. Research local clubs and associations: Search online or ask other business owners in your community about local clubs and associations that align with your industry or interests.
2. Attend meetings: Attend meetings and events to meet other members and learn about new opportunities.
3. Apply for membership: Apply for membership and pay any required fees or dues.
4. Get involved: Volunteer for committees or leadership positions to make connections and gain valuable experience.

Why Attending Networking Events are Important

Attending networking events can help you meet other entrepreneurs and potential customers, and gain valuable insights and resources. Here's why attending networking events are important:

- Networking events provide an opportunity to meet new people and expand your professional network.
- Networking events allow you to build relationships with other entrepreneurs and potential customers

which can lead to new business opportunities and collaborations.

- You gain knowledge from other business owner's experiences and industry experts at networking events and gain valuable insights and resources.
- Expand your network: Networking events help you expand your professional network and connect with people who can help grow your business.

How to Discover Resources

There are many resources available to help you start and grow your business. Here are some tips on how to discover resources:

- Search online for resources related to your industry or business type.
- Contact local economic development organizations, small business development centers, or chambers of commerce to learn about resources in your area.
- Attend workshops and seminars to learn about new tools and strategies for growing your business.

CONCLUSION

Starting a business as a teenager can be both exciting and daunting. The idea of creating something from scratch and bringing it to life is empowering, but the process of getting there can be overwhelming. However, with the right guidance and approach, starting a business can be a fulfilling and rewarding experience.

We've covered some of the key steps involved in starting a business as a teenager. We also explore the importance of identifying your passions and interests, conducting market research, developing a business plan, and brainstorming business name and domain name ideas. These are all critical steps that will set you up for success as you launch your business. But beyond these practical steps, there are a few key principles that we want to emphasize.

First and foremost, *it's important to approach starting a business with a growth mindset*. This means being open to learning, experimenting, and making mistakes. Starting a business is a journey, and it's important to approach it as a learning experience.

Secondly, *it's important to prioritize ethics and integrity in your business*. As a young entrepreneur, you have the opportunity to set a positive example and make a meaningful impact. Make sure that your business is aligned with your values and that you prioritize ethical practices in all aspects of your business.

Finally, *don't forget to have fun*! Starting a business can be a lot of work, but it's also a chance to pursue something that you're passionate about. Enjoy the process, celebrate your successes, and learn from your failures. With the right mindset and approach, starting a business as a teenager can be an incredibly rewarding experience.

Remember, *entrepreneurship is not just about starting a business; it's a mindset and a way of life*. You have the power to create something meaningful, to make a difference, and to achieve your dreams. By following the steps outlined in this book and staying true to your values, you can turn your passion into a successful business and a fulfilling career. So go ahead, take that first step, and let your entrepreneurial journey begin!

About the Author

Tocarra Eldridge-Robinson is the President and founder of federally recognized 501(c)(3) tax-exempt non-profit organization, Still I Rise, which educates, inspires and empowers amongst youth and young adults to obtain self-sufficiency and confidence to ultimately make a positive difference in society. This innovative organization provides entrepreneurial and leadership development programming, along with invaluable mentoring to thousands of diverse youth and young adults via comprehensive and cohesive programs. Additionally, the organization feeds and clothes the homeless and those in need on a monthly basis. Still I Rise has been recognized frequently since its founding in 2014. Awards and honors include: 2021 Kankakee County Chamber of Commerce Nonprofit of the Year Award, 2021 NAACP President's Award, 2019 and 2022 Best of Kankakee Awards.

Robinson is extremely passionate about giving back to her community, as she also serves on various Boards and Committees. Her significant leadership skills are continuously displayed as she continues to be a successful and resourceful instrument to the business world. Driven by her passion for volunteerism and community activism, she works with a multitude of organizations and businesses, and also plays a significant role advocating for community change while working with Congressional and Political leaders, Scholars and Career experts. She frequently volunteers her time to several non-profit organizations, foundations, and community initiatives. Annually, Robinson volunteers for NBA Hall of Famer, Isiah Thomas', annual toy drive.

Robinson is currently pursuing a Doctorate degree in Organizational Leadership. She is a graduate of Roosevelt University, where she earned her Master's degree in Public Administration, as she also interned for Congressman Danny K. Davis. Robinson earned her Bachelor of Arts degree in Criminal Justice from Governors State University. In her initial undergraduate studies, she double majored, earning both, an Associate of Arts degree in Criminal Justice and an Associate of Science degree in Law Enforcement.

She is the driving force behind a multitude of successful innovative businesses in her community. Robinson often consults individuals who desire to become established non-profit organization leaders, which lead her to write and release her book 'How To Start a Non-profit Organization'.

Outside of being a non-profit organization leader, Robinson is also a remarkable journalist whom has interviewed a massive amount of prominent individuals. While promoting her positive energy, she has worked alongside and interviewed industry greats including Danny Glover, Jeff Foxworthy, David and Tamela Mann and a host of more. Additionally, Robinson is a talk show host and professional recording artist.

ABOUT ROBINSON PUBLISHING LLC

Founded in 2018, Robinson Publishing, LLC is an in-house publishing company that publishes, distributes and sells paperback and eBooks. Our books contain valuable content and information that inspire and empower our readers. Some of the Book types include Non-Fiction, Autobiographies, How-To Books, Guides, Poem Books and Children's Books. Robinson Publishing, LLC was derived from magazine publishing, where we successfully published and released national and international magazines since 2014. We expanded our brand to captivate a more diverse audience and avid book readers. We pride ourselves in quality and perfection. We have highly educated, experienced, aspiring and great authors and writers that are knowledgeable in their respected area of profession which makes us a unique company set apart from others.

Robinson Publishing, LLC
Contact: (312) 715-7884